The Resurrection of the Lord Jesus Christ

Algernon J Pollock

Edited by John D Rice

Scripture Truth Publications

THE RESURRECTION OF THE LORD JESUS CHRIST

First published 1947 by The Central Bible Truth Depôt, 11, Little Britain, London, E.C.1.
Revised, re-typeset and transferred to Digital Printing 2015
Second edition July 2015
ISBN: 978-0-901860-94-1 (paperback)
Copyright © 1947 The Central Bible Truth Depôt
Copyright © 2015 John D Rice and Scripture Truth Publications

All rights reserved. No part of this publication may be reproduced, stored in a retrieval system, or transmitted, in any form or by any means, electronic, mechanical, photocopying, recording or otherwise without prior permission of Scripture Truth Publications.

Scripture quotations, unless otherwise indicated, are taken from the New King James Version®. Copyright © 1982 by Thomas Nelson, Inc. Used by permission. All rights reserved.

Scripture quotations marked (KJV) are taken from The Authorized (King James) Version. Rights in the Authorized Version are vested in the Crown. Reproduced by permission of the Crown's patentee, Cambridge University Press.

Cover photograph ©iStockphoto.com/ratluk

Published by Scripture Truth Publications
31-33 Glover Street, Crewe, Cheshire, CW1 3LD

Scripture Truth is an imprint of Central Bible Hammond Trust, a charitable trust

Typesetting by John Rice
Printed and bound by Lightning Source

Foreword

When we were asked to recommend a book to accompany a summer conference for young people on the subject of the resurrection of the Lord Jesus Christ, our thoughts turned quickly to A J Pollock's pamphlet on the subject, long out of print. After asking others to read it through, it became apparent that, although the subject matter was very relevant, its impact was blunted by words and phrases no longer in everyday use. This edition retains the structure, argument and scriptural references of the original, but presented in twenty-first century language.

As you read, may the wonder of the resurrection deepen your appreciation of the One who once died but now lives in the power of an endless life.

John Rice

July 2015

THE RESURRECTION OF THE LORD JESUS CHRIST

Contents

                                                            Page

Foreword 3

Introduction 7

The Resurrection of Christ Stated 11

The Old Testament Prophesied
     the Resurrection of Christ 14

The Lord Jesus Prophesied
     His Own Resurrection 17

Three Immensely Great Considerations 21

The Resurrection of Our Lord Jesus Christ . . 26

The Witness to Our Lord's Resurrection 31

To Whom Did Our Lord Appear? 40

The Sign of the Prophet Jonah 43

Were the Four Records
     of the Resurrection of Christ Inspired? . . 49

The Conversion of the Apostle Paul 53

The Testimony of the Epistles
     to the Resurrection of Christ 56

Lies and Theories 61

Observations on the Conversion
     and Apostleship of St. Paul 66

The Best Authenticated Fact in All History . . 83

THE RESURRECTION OF THE LORD JESUS CHRIST

Introduction

What would you think, if you attended the funeral of a very dear friend on a Friday, and you met him walking down the street alive and well the following Sunday, and he informed you that he had risen from the dead that very morning? Such an occurrence would doubtless give you a tremendous shake. It would not be surprising, if you fell down in a faint, and, when you recovered, your mind would be in a state of indescribable agitation.

And further, having met your friend more than once during the succeeding days, so that no doubt remained in your mind of the reality of his resurrection, what would your feelings be, if you were told that while he was talking to a group of friends, he suddenly began to leave this earth, the friends testifying how they saw him disappear in a cloud? Your mind would certainly be left in a state of whirling tumult.

You reply that such an occurrence could not possibly take place. You are quite right in your reply, except for

one great exception,

besides which there can be none other. Such an incident did really happen. It is an historical fact that the Lord

Jesus Christ actually rose from the dead, and ascended up to heaven.

We use the above illustration with the deepest reverence, seeking to prepare the minds of our readers to realize the stupendous character of the resurrection of our Lord; and further to give them some little sympathy with the disciples in their slowness to receive the testimony that our Lord had risen from the dead, seeing there was nothing like His resurrection in past history. And nothing quite like it will ever happen again. It stands out in all its divine significance, opening the door of hope to a sin-blighted, death-ridden world of sinful people.

The Bible gives instances of two men — Enoch and Elijah — being translated to heaven without dying at all; of some dead people, who were raised to life, only to die again; but we never read of a resurrected man ascending to heaven, save in the one exception of our Lord. He died, and was raised the third day, and having abundantly proved His resurrection to His doubting disciples, He ascended to glory, and set Himself down at the right hand of God. Such a claim is stupendous. Prove it, and you prove Christianity. Disprove it, and you disprove Christianity. The truth of Christianity hinges on the fact of the resurrection of our Lord.

This was seen in the remarkable case of Lord Lyttleton, a brilliant literary man, a former Chancellor of the Exchequer, and his friend, Gilbert West. They lived in the early part of the eighteenth century, were both lawyers, and, as the fashion then was, were deists. Deists admit the fact of a Creator, but hold that once the creation is formed, the Creator retired from any further activity in this world's concerns. They therefore did not believe in

INTRODUCTION

revealed religion, in the Bible, in Christ, in the need for salvation.

These gentlemen conceived the idea, that if they could succeed in disproving the resurrection of Christ, it would administer an absolute death-blow to Christianity — that it could not possibly survive the exposure. Lord Lyttleton therefore attempted to prove that the alleged conversion of the Apostle Paul was a fraud, while Gilbert West tried to prove that the resurrection of Christ never occurred.

These two lawyers set to work to study what the Scriptures have to say on these subjects. It can safely be affirmed that generally speaking destructive critics of the Bible are very ignorant of its contents, upon which they dare to sit in judgment. Not only so, but some start with a strong contrary bias, that blinds them, wishing to put the Bible in the wrong. It was so in this case, Lord Lyttleton and Gilbert West hoping to overthrow Christianity, and to exult over the defeat of the Christians.

Being lawyers, and well trained in the weighing of evidence, they found to their astonishment the evidence as to the resurrection of Christ unassailable, and the conversion of the Apostle Paul manifestly true. How often has it been that people, who come to scoff, remain to pray. It was so in this case, for instead of writing to disprove the truth of the resurrection of Christ, they wrote as being fully convinced of its truth, carrying with it their acknowledgment of the great truths of the Christian faith.

The writer hopes in the latter part of this pamphlet to reproduce in his own language some of Lord Lyttleton's arguments, which will convince the reader of his wisdom in the selection of the subject he chose; or rather, as we think, that the Spirit of God guided him unwittingly to choose with such happy result.

THE RESURRECTION OF THE LORD JESUS CHRIST

We trust the mind of the reader is now prepared to give the closest attention to what we shall bring forward from the Word of God on this vital theme.

The Resurrection of Christ Stated

In the Scriptures the resurrection of Christ is stated in so many words over seventy times, whilst the teaching and moral effects that flow from this great fact are woven throughout the fabric of the New Testament epistles. The details of the resurrection of our Lord are given historically and circumstantially in the four Gospels. Later on in the Acts of the Apostles and the Epistles we read such sample Scriptures as the following:

> "With great power the apostles gave *witness to the resurrection of the Lord Jesus.* And great grace was upon them all" (Acts 4:33).

* * * * *

> "Christ was *raised from the dead* by the glory of the Father" (Romans 6:4).

A whole chapter of fifty-eight verses — 1 Corinthians 15 — is devoted to stating the resurrection of our Lord, and the consequence flowing from it, namely, the resurrection of the saints at the second coming of our Lord. The seriousness of denying the resurrection of Christ is seen in the solemn warning,

"*If Christ is **not** risen*, your faith is futile; you are still in your sins!" (1 Corinthians 15:17).

In the ordinance of Christian baptism we get the resurrection of our Lord particularly emphasized:

"If we have been united together in the likeness of His death, certainly we also shall be *in the likeness of His resurrection*" (Romans 6:5).

The resurrection of our Lord was put forward as a great outstanding fact in the sermon that the Apostle Peter preached on the great day of Pentecost:

"This Jesus *God has raised up*, of which we are all witnesses" (Acts 2:32).

It was likewise the theme of the Apostle Paul's testimony when he preached to the Epicurean and Stoic philosophers on Mars Hill at Athens. He warned his hearers in very solemn language, that

"God has appointed a day on which He will judge the world in righteousness by the Man whom He has ordained. He has given assurance of this to all *by raising Him from the dead*" (Acts 17:31).

Here we find the resurrection of Christ is the solemn assurance to all people of coming judgment. Who then can stand? On the other hand the resurrection of Christ is very vital to believers.

"If you confess with your mouth the Lord Jesus and believe in your heart that *God has raised Him from the dead*, you will be saved" (Romans 10:9).

Apart from the resurrection of Christ there can be no salvation, no forgiveness of sins, no justification, and no gift of eternal life — in short, no Christianity. Remove the central stone of an arch, and the whole structure falls to the ground. So it is with the Deity and Manhood of our Lord Jesus Christ, His spotless life, His atoning death, His resurrection, His ascension. These are all linked up together, making one complete whole. If one part fails, the whole of Christianity fails.

The Old Testament Prophesied the Resurrection of Christ

We'll look at three prophetic Scriptures which plainly speak of the Messiah.

PSALM 16

We read,

> "You will not leave My soul in Sheol [the unseen world], nor will You allow Your Holy One to see corruption. You will show Me the path of life; in Your presence is fullness of joy; at Your right hand are pleasures for evermore" (Psalm 16:10-11).

This Scripture most plainly implies resurrection. The Apostle Peter in his famous pentecostal sermon argued that this could not have applied to David, the writer of the psalm, for he had been dead and buried for long years, and his tomb was well-known to that day. So he plainly stated,

> "He [David], foreseeing this, spoke concerning the resurrection of the **Christ**, that His soul was not left in Hades, nor did His flesh see corruption. *This*

THE OLD TESTAMENT PROPHESIED THE RESURRECTION

Jesus God has raised up, of which we are all witnesses" (Acts 2:31-32).

PSALM 22

A thousand years before our Lord died upon the cross, we have in this psalm a vivid prophecy of the crucifixion, beginning with the bitter cry of anguish our Lord uttered in His abandonment by God when He took the sinner's place.

> "My God, My God, why have You forsaken Me?" (verse 1).

When the psalmist wrote the words,

> "You have brought Me to the dust of death" (verse 15),

he evidently was not referring to his own death, for he was still alive when he wrote the psalm, but prophetically of our Lord's atoning death on the cross of Calvary. The psalm then goes on to say,

> "I will declare Your name *to My brethren*; in the midst of the assembly I will praise You" (verse 22).

For this to come to pass resurrection was necessary.

ISAIAH 53

We read,

> "He [*referring to the Christ to come*] was taken from prison and from judgment, and who will declare His generation? For He was cut off from the land of the living; for the transgressions of My people He was stricken" (Isaiah 53:8).

This most plainly prophesied our Lord's atoning death on the cross. Yet *after that* we read,

"When You make His soul an offering for sin, *He shall see His seed*, He shall prolong His days, and the pleasure of the Lord shall prosper in His hand" (Isaiah 53:10).

Here we have the resurrection of our Lord plainly implied, the holy triumph of our Lord over sin and death and hell amply set forth.

It is well to stress these prophetic Scriptures as proving the foreknowledge of God centuries before the events materialized. It is easy for critics to charge the many witnesses to our Lord's resurrection with lying, but it would be beyond even their audacity to claim that the Old Testament prophets were lying, men who lived centuries apart, and having no knowledge of what each other wrote. It would be strange if men with no knowledge of each other, should all without collusion on their part be found to be lying on one particular point. On the face of it this would be an impossible thing. And if their prophecies materialized, as they surely did, it establishes the truthfulness of the New Testament witnesses to the resurrection of our Lord, as it does their own witness.

The Lord Jesus Prophesied His Own Resurrection

In this our Lord was unique. No one in all the history of the world, save Himself, prophesied this. Hear His own words,

> "The Son of Man will be betrayed to the chief priests and to the scribes; and they will condemn Him to death, and deliver Him to the Gentiles to mock and to scourge and to crucify. And the third day *He will rise again*" (Matthew 20:18-19).

* * * * *

> "He [the Lord Jesus] taught His disciples and said to them, 'The Son of Man is being betrayed into the hands of men, and they will kill Him. And after He is killed, *He will rise the third day*'" (Mark 9:31).

* * * * *

> "Then He [the Lord Jesus] took the twelve aside and said to them, 'Behold, we are going up to Jerusalem, and all things that are written by the prophets concerning the Son of Man will be accomplished. For He will be delivered to the

Gentiles and will be mocked and insulted and spit upon. They will scourge Him and kill Him. *And the third day He will rise again*'" (Luke 18:31-33).

Either our Lord was what He said He was, and the fulfilment of this prophecy would prove it, or else He was the most consummate blasphemer and liar the world has ever known. Shall Christianity owe its success to a lie? Can good fruit be born on a rotten tree? For what are the fruits of Christianity, but what people generally praise and admire? Even infidels and sceptics, who reject the claims of Christ, and deny His resurrection, write of His moral character in terms of glowing praise. Can they do this consistently, believing Christ to be an imposter? Surely not, or else they fail to see how incongruous they are to praise our Lord's moral excellence on the one hand, and on the other hand to disbelieve His claims as to His deity, His true manhood, and the atoning character of His death, which, if untrue, were indeed blasphemous assertions.

The late Theodore Parker, a well-known infidel writer in America, wrote,

> "Measure Jesus by the shadow He cast into the world; no, by the light He shed upon it. Shall we be told that such a Person never lived? that the whole story is a lie? Suppose that Plato and Newton had never lived. But who did their works, and thought their thoughts? It takes a Newton to forge a Newton. What man could have fabricated a Jesus? None but Jesus."

We could give elaborate tribute after elaborate tribute of our Lord from infidel pens. Strange to admit so much, and not see, if our Lord did not rise from the dead, that

THE LORD JESUS PROPHESIED HIS OWN RESURRECTION

He was a consummate liar, and instead of being praised, He should have been condemned in the severest terms.

A story is told of the evil days of the French Revolution at the end of the eighteenth century. France at that time threw off the profession of Christianity. A woman was enthroned in mock-royal robes in the cathedral of Notre Dame, Paris, as the Goddess of Reason. The Lord's Day was abolished, and in its place a holiday was substituted every tenth day. A deistical system of religion was drawn up by the French Directory (1796), designed to supplant Christianity.

But this new religion — *theophilanthropy* {friendship with God and man} — did not become popular with the masses. At that time there was a famous statesman, who had previously been a bishop in the Catholic Church, Talleyrand by name. He was talking with the leaders of this new religion, who were deploring its lack of success. To their astonishment Talleyrand said, "Gentlemen, I can tell you how to make your new religion succeed, and that without lavish expenditure." They eagerly asked to be let into the secret. He replied, "Let one of your number be crucified and put to death, buried, and rise again the third day. Let this happen, and your religion will succeed."

But here was One, who not only rose from the dead, but before His death prophesied His own resurrection; and not only so, but prophets long centuries before foretold the same. Could this have been brought about by the cleverness of man, or by human arrangement? Impossible!

We know that the Old Testament Scriptures were written hundreds of years before Christ was born into the world. There is no disputing that. What then made Moses, David, Isaiah and others prophesy the coming of our Lord into this world? Moreover, these ancient prophecies have been fulfilled. Can you explain this, save on the ground of inspiration?

Three Immensely Great Considerations

Before we come to the examination of what Scripture teaches as to the resurrection of our Lord, it will be helpful for the better understanding of that supreme event to consider three things in their inter-relation one to the other. It is natural to ask, **Who** is it that could rise from the dead? What kind of life was it, that deserved such a distinction? What character was the death that could claim resurrection? Let us consider then:

(1) *The Person, who rose from the dead;*

(2) *The character of His life;*

(3) *The character of His death.*

All these are intimately connected with our Lord's resurrection in the scheme of Christianity. Without a right perspective of these, and their inter-relationship one with the other, we shall not be in a position to understand rightly the supremely important nature of the resurrection of Christ, and the immense results that have flowed from that fact from that day to this.

Everything about the Lord is vital. We may have a differing opinion about this great person and that great person, and in the end our opinion would make little difference. But in the case of our Lord, He claimed that He alone could bring people into right relationship with God for their eternal blessing. If this claim is true, it is vital to every one of us; if false, it reaches the highest point of blasphemy possible.

THE PERSON OF THE LORD JESUS CHRIST

There must be something extraordinarily special in the person of our Lord, seeing His resurrection carries with it such far-reaching results. It is very striking that the Apostle John in his wonderful Gospel presents Christ as the only begotten Son of God — One eternally with the Father and the Holy Spirit in the unity of the Godhead. Scripture declares that He always was the eternal Word, and that as the Word He was *with* God (that is, a distinct Person in the Godhead); *and was Himself God*, even as the Father is God, and the Holy Spirit is God, yet **one** God (John 1:1-2).

And this Divine Person became Man. We read these amazing words:

> "And the Word became flesh and dwelt among us, and we beheld His glory, the glory as of the only begotten of the Father, full of grace and truth" (John 1:14).

With such a Person before us, everything relating to Him is lifted far above that which marks the greatest and wisest of people. We are not surprised that He was characterized by actions perfectly unique to Himself, and quite unlike that which happens to people generally.

THE CHARACTER OF OUR LORD'S LIFE

Why did the eternal Son of God become Man? It was because *by man* sin entered into the world, and death by sin, and therefore the penalty of sin must be met *by man* in order to give a holy God a righteous basis for offering forgiveness of sins and eternal life to guilty people (Romans 5:18). What man was sufficient for this? It is evident that the One, who could do this, must Himself be perfectly sinless, One upon whom death had no claim. And who could fulfil that condition? Look at the millions of the human race. Is there one untainted by sin? All are sinners. All need a Saviour. Not one out of the myriad ranks of sinful mankind could come forward to take the sinner's place.

Only One could come forward, and this was the sinless One, the Lord Jesus Christ, the Eternal Son of the Father. He alone could say,

> "Behold, I have come — in the volume of the book it is written of Me — to do Your will, O God" (Hebrews 10:7).

This is why our Lord became Man, yet never ceasing to be the eternal Son in the unity of the Godhead with the Father and the Holy Spirit.

With delight we follow the record of His blameless, spotless life as Man on this earth. He was perfectly sinless in thought, word and deed. He never apologized for anything He said or did, for there never was the slightest occasion for His so doing. He never retreated from any position He ought to have taken up. In fullest measure He ever did His Father's will. Here was One, the like of whom before or since the world has never seen. He was

> "God manifest in the flesh" (1 Timothy 3:16).

His life as Man was never, in any particular, in contradiction to His Godhead glory. All was in complete harmony.

The Character of Our Lord's Death

And yet it was not His holy blameless life that could save people from the penalty of their sins. Unless He had been sinless, He could not have been the sinner's Saviour, yet Scripture teaches us that it is not His life that saves, *but His **atoning** death*, and that alone. Scripture lays great emphasis on our Lord's death.

> "Without shedding of blood there is no remission" (Hebrews 9:22).

*   *   *   *   *

> "The blood of Jesus Christ His Son cleanses us from all sin" (1 John 1:7).

All the righteous judgment of God against sin was poured out on the holy Person of our Lord Jesus Christ, as He hung upon the cross of Calvary. Within those three hours of holy suffering when there was darkness over all the land, our Lord's great victory over sin, death and hell was accomplished. There and there only did "mercy and truth" meet; there and there only did "righteousness and peace" kiss each other (Psalm 85:10). There only could be heard the loud triumphant cry,

> **"It is finished!"** (John 19:30).

God can now righteously and gloriously forgive any sinner, who truly puts his trust in the Saviour, who

> "suffered once for sins, the Just for the unjust, that He might bring us to God" (1 Peter 3:18).

The Christian ordinance of baptism lays emphatic stress upon the death of our Lord Jesus Christ.

> "Do you not know that as many of us as were baptized into Christ Jesus were baptized *into His death*?" (Romans 6:3).

The Christian ordinance of the Lord's supper, likewise, lays emphatic stress on the death of our Lord Jesus Christ.

> "As often as you eat this bread and drink this cup, you proclaim *the Lord's death* till He comes" (1 Corinthians 11:26).

We miss the whole point of the Scriptures, if we fail to realize that our Lord's death was absolutely unique, that no one has ever died a death like His, that no other person could experience such a death, for it was an atoning sacrificial death, absolutely necessary for man's salvation.

These few thoughts as to the Person who rose from the dead, the character of His life, and of His death, may lead the reader to a fuller understanding of the significance of His resurrection, and to see that it is all consistent with what He is and what He has done, all falling into beautiful harmony, and bearing on it the stamp of truth.

The Resurrection of Our Lord Jesus Christ

After our Lord died we read that,

> "Joseph of Arimathæa, a prominent council member, who was himself waiting for the kingdom of God, coming and taking courage, went in to Pilate and asked for the body of Jesus" (Mark 15:43).

Pilate had publicly declared at the trial of our Lord that he found no fault in Him, and yet, bowing before the fanaticism of the Jews on the one hand, and moved by fear that he might not stand well with Cæsar if he allowed One who claimed to be the King of the Jews to live, to his eternal shame he gave sentence that it should be as His enemies required (Luke 23:24).

Was there ever such a barefaced travesty of justice? What judge would dare to permit the clamour of the accusers to settle the verdict, especially when the sentence was a death sentence? Pilate passing the death sentence, yet declaring that he found no fault in our Lord, made the Gentiles guilty. The Jews clamouring for His death made the Jews guilty.

THE RESURRECTION OF OUR LORD JESUS CHRIST

Once our Lord had glorified God in His sacrificial atoning death on the cross of Calvary, no *unbelieving* hand was allowed to touch Him. In this we see the overruling hand of God in that Pilate gave leave to Joseph of Arimathæa to remove the body of our Lord, and give it burial, fulfilling a seven-century old prophecy that our Lord would lie "with the rich in His death" (Isaiah 53:9).

Joseph with Nicodemus, this latter until then a secret believer, performed this last act of grateful, loving homage to our Lord. A hundred {Roman} pounds weight [about 75lb or 34kg] of myrrh and aloes was brought to the grave. The holy body of our Lord was swathed in linen clothes with the spices, and was reverently laid in Joseph's new tomb, in which nobody had previously been laid. The women, too, who accompanied our Lord from Galilee, followed after, and saw the tomb, and where the body was laid.

Previously the Jews, in view of the next day being "the day after the Sabbath", and that Sabbath being a high day, had gone to Pilate to ask that the bodies of those who had been crucified should not remain on their crosses, requesting him that their legs should be broken, thus expediting their death, and their removal from the crosses. To this end the legs of the two thieves were broken, but when they came to our Lord they found Him dead already. This was the fulfilment of a prophecy,

> "Not one of His bones shall be broken" (John 19:36).

But, as if to make assurance doubly sure, a Roman soldier took his spear, and pierced the side of the dead Christ, and immediately there came out blood and water.

THE RESURRECTION OF THE LORD JESUS CHRIST

A ROMAN GUARD KEPT WATCH OVER OUR LORD'S TOMB

The wicked fanaticism of the Jews followed our Lord even after His death. We read:

> "The chief priests and Pharisees gathered together to Pilate, saying, 'Sir, we remember, while He was still alive, how that deceiver said, "After three days I will rise." Therefore command that the tomb be made secure until the third day, lest His disciples come by night and steal Him away, and say to the people, "He has risen from the dead." So the last deception will be worse than the first'" (Matthew 27:62-64).

Pilate granted their request. A guard of Roman soldiers was detailed to watch the tomb, whilst the Jews with the authority of Pilate sealed the great stone, rolled against its mouth. The next day being the Sabbath the sorrowing disciples rested according to the commandment (Luke 23:56).

"THE DAY AFTER THE SABBATH"

Then came the eventful day, the third day after the crucifixion, the day our Lord prophesied He would rise from the dead. Would His words prove to be true?

Heaven stepped in. What was a seal upon the mouth of the tomb compared to Divine power? The puny hand of man was brushed aside. We read,

> "An angel of the Lord descended from heaven, and came and rolled back the stone from the door, and sat on it. His countenance was like lightning, and his clothing as white as snow. And the guards shook for fear of him, and became like dead men" (Matthew 28:2-4).

It must have been a truly terrifying sight. The guard became as dead men, that is they fainted, and became unconscious through sheer terror. Heaven broke the seal that man put upon the tomb; but, mark it well, not to let the Saviour out of the tomb, *but to let us look in*. When the tomb was looked in upon, it was to find no body of our Lord, but the linen clothes lying, and the napkin that was about His sacred head wrapped together in a place by itself. He, who could pass through closed doors on the first day after His resurrection, could surely rise out of the tomb in spite of its thick walls. Unseen by mortal eye, He rose in wondrous power, raised by the glory of the Father, deliberately leaving the linen clothes with which He was wrapped, and putting the head napkin in a place by itself, all indicating nothing hurried, but of His being completely Master of the situation. No, the stone was rolled away by angelic might, the seal was broken, we repeat, not to let the Saviour out, but to let us look in, and to testify to us how He had broken the power of sin and death and hell.

Recovering from their faint some of the guard went into the city and reported to the chief priests the extraordinary events that had taken place. This we will comment on more fully later.

The Empty Tomb

Meanwhile Mary Magdalene, Joanna (the wife of Chuza, Herod's steward), Mary, the mother of our Lord, and other women from Galilee came early to the tomb, bringing spices, only to find the stone rolled away. Entering the tomb they did not find the body of the Lord Jesus. The angel reassured the sorrowing women telling them not to fear, saying,

THE RESURRECTION OF THE LORD JESUS CHRIST

"He is not here; for He is risen, as He said. Come, see the place where the Lord lay" (Matthew 28:6).

He then urged them to carry news of our Lord's resurrection to His disciples, telling them to meet Him in Galilee. With great joy they ran to deliver this wonderful message, but their words seemed to the disciples like nonsense, and they refused to believe that our Lord was risen from the dead. It is a strong point in the proof of the resurrection of our Lord that the disciples were slow to believe, and refused to acknowledge the fact of the Lord's resurrection till they had indisputable, first-hand proof. If they had been credulous, eager to believe any tale they heard, one could understand their testimony would have had no weight, but when disciples, slow to believe the astounding news of our Lord's resurrection, were convinced of its truth by indisputable evidences, their testimony should not be denied. We read that our Lord showed Himself alive

> "**by many infallible proofs**, being seen by them [His disciples] during forty days and speaking of the things pertaining to the kingdom of God" (Acts 1:3).

The Apostles Peter and John then went to the tomb to see if the report of the women was correct. In their eagerness they ran, but John, the younger man, outran Peter. John contented himself by looking into the tomb, but Peter, marked by impetuosity, went inside the tomb, seeing the linen clothes lying, and the head napkin in a place by itself, and they returned to their own homes.

The Witness to Our Lord's Resurrection

We shall see as we proceed that the number of the witnesses to our Lord's resurrection, and the details which each one was able to provide, constitute a growing body of evidence that cannot be set aside. To refuse their witness we should have to write them all off as liars, and, going back to Old Testament prophecies of the resurrection of Christ centuries before the event, we should also have to brand Moses, David, Isaiah, Micah and other Old Testament prophets as liars also, though they were separated by centuries, and did not know what each other wrote. It is beyond all experience and reason that they should all be found lying. Moreover, what could they gain by witnessing to the resurrection of our Lord, but persecutions, imprisonments and martyrdoms? What could the followers of the Crucified expect but the world's bitter opposition?

The First Appearance of the Risen Christ

In spite of the emphatic declaration of the angels, Mary Magdalene could not fully believe that the Lord was indeed risen from the dead. One can understand this, and sympathize with her feelings. The experience was so utterly unique. Nothing like it had been known in all the history of the world. Reluctant to leave the spot where her Lord had been buried, standing by the tomb weeping, she glanced into the tomb, and saw two angels sitting, one at the head, and the other at the feet where the body of the Lord had lain. They asked her the reason for her tears. She replied it was because they had taken away the body of her Lord, and she did not know where they had laid it.

Turning back, behold! the risen Lord stood before her. She did not recognize Him at first, perhaps the dimness of the early morning light, and being blinded by her tears, may have accounted for this. She supposed Him to be the gardener. Our Lord asked why she wept, and for whom she was seeking? She replied with the deep affection that ever marked her, that, if the body of the Lord had been taken away, and He would tell her where it was laid, she would take it away, little realizing in the strength of her affections, the weakness of her body for such an impossible task.

Our Lord turned round, and uttered the one word, Mary. Instantly she recognized her Lord, replying Rabboni, that is to say, Master. Then the Lord commissioned her to carry that most wonderful message to the disciples:

> "Go to My brethren and say to them, 'I am ascending to My Father and your Father, and to My God and your God'" (John 20:17).

THE SECOND APPEARANCE OF THE RISEN CHRIST

This was to the women, who, when they arrived at the tomb early on the morning of the first day of the week, were told by the angel that the Lord was risen from the dead, and who sent by them a message to the disciples **and Peter** that He was risen, and that He would go before them to Galilee, and meet them there (Mark 16:7). As they went on this errand, the Lord met them on the way. In their joy they held Him by His feet, and worshipped Him. As they thus handled Him they knew it was no apparition that stood before them, but their loved Lord risen from the dead.

It is very touching that when the angel sent this message to His disciples, he should have added the words, "and Peter". Was not Peter included among the disciples? Why mention him specially? Peter, after his frightful backsliding, might well have wondered if he were included in the message. But this addition, "and Peter", would set his mind at rest, and give him fresh courage to face his Lord. Here we find the tender compassion of the Good Shepherd shining forth in the wording of the angel's message.

THE THIRD APPEARANCE OF THE RISEN CHRIST

This was to Peter, evidently following up the message, "*and Peter*". No one knows what passed between them at that interview, but again we mark the tenderness and compassion of the Good Shepherd, the Great Shepherd risen from the dead (Hebrews 13:20). Comparing 1 Corinthians 15:5 with Luke 24:34, this is made plain. We read:

> "The Lord is risen indeed, *and has appeared to Simon!*"

We gather that Peter was seen by our Lord before He saw the eleven on the evening of the first day of the week, when He rose from the dead. This care of our Lord for His wandering sheep is surely an encouragement to every backslider to seek the Lord afresh, and feel that, if He could and did restore such a backslider as Peter, He can restore any backslider.

THE RESURRECTION OF THE LORD JESUS CHRIST

THE FOURTH APPEARANCE OF THE RISEN CHRIST

This was to Cleopas and his companion, probably his wife, when on their way to their home in the village of Emmaus. The risen Lord drew near to them, their eyes prevented from recognising Him. He asked the reason of their sadness, as they talked by the way. With astonishment they asked, Was He only a stranger in Jerusalem, and had He not heard of the wonderful happenings that had taken place? Our Lord enquired what things? They replied,

> "Concerning Jesus of Nazareth, who was a Prophet mighty in deed and word before God and all the people, and how the chief priests and our rulers delivered Him to be condemned to death, and crucified Him. But we were hoping that it was He who was going to redeem Israel. Indeed, besides all this, today is the third day since these things happened" (Luke 24:19-21).

They then went on to say that certain of their company had gone to the tomb, and had found it empty, and had heard the angel's testimony that the Lord was risen.

As they walked towards Emmaus, our Lord opened up to them the Scriptures, and showed them how, centuries before, the Old Testament prophets had foretold that He would suffer, and then enter into His glory. Their hearts burned within them, as they listened to His marvellous unfolding of their Old Testament prophecies; so much so, that they invited Him to stay with them that night, for it was getting late. At their humble meal, in the breaking of bread, He was made known to them. Did they note, we wonder, the scars in His hands? They recognized Him with a deep thrill of joy, and then just when they had recognized Him, He vanished out of their sight.

Once they knew that the Lord was risen, everything was changed for them. In sadness they began their long walk to Emmaus, troubled and perplexed; in joy and glad assurance they retraced their steps to Jerusalem to share the good news with the eleven disciples, only to hear that the Lord had already appeared to Simon.

THE FIFTH APPEARANCE OF THE RISEN CHRIST

As the two disciples from Emmaus broke into the room where the eleven disciples were gathered together, to hear how the Lord had appeared to Simon, we read,

> "Now as they said these things, Jesus Himself stood in the midst of them, and said to them, 'Peace to you.' But they were terrified and frightened, and supposed they had seen a spirit. And He said to them, 'Why are you troubled? And why do doubts arise in your hearts? Behold My hands and My feet, that it is I Myself. Handle Me and see, for a spirit does not have flesh and bones as you see I have.' When He had said this, He showed them His hands and His feet. But while they still did not believe for joy, and marvelled, He said to them, 'Have you any food here?' So they gave Him a piece of a broiled fish and some honeycomb. And He took it and ate in their presence" (Luke 24:36-43).

From this narrative we gather two things:

- that the disciples were incredulous and slow to believe, and required strong proofs before they would be convinced of the resurrection of our Lord;
- that the Lord graciously gave them the strongest proofs that He was indeed the risen Christ.

He showed them His hands and feet with the marks of the nails. He invited them to handle Him, so that they might be assured that He was no apparition. Then further He took the initiative, asking them if they had any food, and He graciously ate in their presence. Surely proofs could not have been fuller and more convincing than these.

We have purposely given the above Scripture showing this in full. What room was left for doubt? The reaction in the minds of the disciples was very marked. They could not believe for real joy. Moreover, He reminded them that He had foretold His resurrection when He was with them, and how all that was written in the law of Moses, the prophets and the psalms concerning Him was all fulfilled (Luke 24:44-46). Surely proof could not have been more complete and satisfying.

THE SIXTH APPEARANCE OF THE RISEN CHRIST

On His previous appearance to His disciples one of them, Thomas surnamed Didymus, was not present. Hearing their testimony of the appearance of our Lord in the midst of His own, he stoutly affirmed that he would not believe in the resurrection of the Lord, unless he could put his finger into the print of the nails in His hands, and thrust his hand into His side. A week later the Lord again appeared to His disciples, this time Thomas being present. Our Lord said to him,

> "Reach your finger here, and look at My hands; and reach your hand here, and put it into My side. Do not be unbelieving, but believing" (John 20:27).

How gracious and patient was the Lord in thus overcoming the unwillingness of His doubting disciple to believe. How confirming it must have been to the others to have His visit to them thus repeated. Thomas, convinced at last, exclaimed in deepest reverence,

> "*My Lord and my God!*" (John 20:28).

The Seventh Appearance of the Risen Christ

The next appearance of our Lord was in Galilee. Peter had declared that He would go a fishing. Six other of the disciples went with Him. They toiled all night at the fishing and caught nothing. When the morning was come, Jesus was standing on the shore. Unrecognized by the disciples, He asked them if they had any fish. Being answered in the negative, He told them to cast their net on the right side of the ship. They did so, enclosing one hundred and fifty-three great fishes, and yet the net did not break (John 21:1-11).

Was this a reminder that our Lord had called His disciples to be fishers of *men*, that when they went back to fishing for fish *they* had caught nothing, yet *at His* word they had ample supplies? Moreover when they got to shore it was to find that the Lord had provided them with a fire of coals, and fish laid on it and bread. Was not our Lord, who had called them to fish for men, sufficient to meet their bodily needs?

The Eighth Appearance of the Risen Christ

This took place when the eleven disciples went to a mountain in Galilee to meet the Lord as He had appointed the first day He rose from the dead. The Apostle Paul tells us of five hundred brothers seeing the Lord at one time (1 Corinthians 15:6). This was probably the occasion to which Paul called attention. That our Lord should make an appointment to meet His disciples would give ample time for notice to be given to many of the disciples, who loved Him, an opportunity to assemble at the appointed meeting place. Up to this point the Lord's appearances were sudden and unexpected, but here was an appointment to meet His disciples on a mountain in Galilee.

It is a further proof of the truth of our narrative, that Paul could say when he wrote about five hundred brothers seeing the Lord at one time, that the majority of them were alive at the time of his writing. The Apostle would not have dared to put forth such a statement, capable of public refutation by so many, if it were not true.

The Ninth Appearance of the Risen Christ

The ninth appearance was to the Apostle James. This we gather from 1 Corinthians 15:7, where it is plain that this interview took place *after* our Lord was seen by five hundred brothers at once, and *before* He saw His disciples for the last time on earth, just before His ascension to the right hand of God. We have no indication of why James had this special interview with the Lord.

The Tenth Appearance of the Risen Christ

Our Lord finally led His disciples out as far as to Bethany. Reaching their destination, with uplifted hands He blessed His disciples. What tenderness these last words on earth must have expressed! Whilst so doing He was parted from them, and carried up into heaven. Two men in white apparel said to the wondering disciples as they stood gazing steadfastly to heaven,

> "Men of Galilee, why do you stand gazing up into heaven? This same Jesus, who was taken up from you into heaven, will so come in like manner as you saw Him go into heaven" (Acts 1:11).

The disciples were left with a wonderful hope. Our Lord promised to send the Holy Spirit of God to indwell them, and provide them with power from on high. He instructed them to wait at Jerusalem till the moment came when this promise should be fulfilled. We read,

THE WITNESS TO OUR LORD'S RESURRECTION

"They worshipped Him, and returned to Jerusalem with great joy, and were continually in the temple praising and blessing God. Amen" (Luke 24:52-53).

To Whom Did Our Lord Appear?

There is one particular point to which we must draw attention. When our Lord rose from the dead, it would have been very convincing if He had suddenly appeared to Pilate, Herod, the chief priests, and the inhabitants of Jerusalem. In such a case surely the evidence to His resurrection could not have been denied. If the narrative had come from the pens of uninspired writers, this would have been the likely story they would have told. On the contrary our Lord's appearances in His risen state were only to His own disciples, to those who loved Him, and not to the world. The Apostle Peter emphasizes this when we read,

> "Him God raised up on the third day, and showed Him openly, not to all the people, but *to witnesses chosen before by God, even to us who ate and drank with Him after He arose from the dead*" (Acts 10: 40-41).

Why was this? Let us lead up to the answer of our question.

It is significant that all through the Lord's public ministry of three-and-a-half years, though the Jews continually plotted to kill Him, He was never subjected to physical injury, until the scene in the Garden of Gethsemane. Our Lord said,

> "When I was with you daily in the temple, you did not try to seize Me. **but this is your hour, and the power of darkness**" (Luke 22:53).

Once that hour came by Divine permission our Lord was subjected to scoffing, the hair plucked off His cheek, His face spit upon, scorn and humiliating treatment were His portion. A reed was put into His hand as a mock sceptre, and a crown of thorns in mockery of a kingly diadem was placed upon His head. Finally He was crucified.

But when He rose from the dead everything was different. Risen from the dead, not a single unbeliever saw Him. Only those who loved and adored Him witnessed Him in His risen state. Why was this? It was because He could say,

> "I did not come to judge the world but to *save* the world" (John 12:47).

If our Lord had *publicly* appeared to His enemies, it would have meant destruction to them. Instead of confronting them with their evil deeds to their utter confusion and destruction, He commissioned His disciples to preach the Gospel, beginning at Jerusalem, the very city of His murderers.

An illustration of this was seen in the time of our Lord's public ministry on earth. The Jews' Feast of Tabernacles was at hand, and our Lord's brothers pressed Him to go up to the feast *publicly*. This He declined to do, for when the Lord presents Himself publicly He will have to take

> "out of His kingdom all things that offend, and those who practice lawlessness, and will cast them

into the furnace of fire. There will be wailing and gnashing of teeth" (Matthew 13:41-42).

If the Lord had gone up *publicly*, and all offenders had been removed, how many would have been left?

But our Lord went up, as it were, *secretly*, thus enabling Him to present Himself *in grace*. Hence He could cry on the last great day of the feast, when lifeless ritualism had left the worshippers empty and unsatisfied,

> "If anyone thirsts, *let him come to **Me** and drink*. He who believes in Me, as the Scripture has said, out of his heart will flow rivers of living water" (John 7:37-38).

When our Lord, as Son of Man, does come *publicly*, we read,

> "Behold, He is coming with clouds, and every eye will see Him, even they who pierced Him. And all the tribes of the earth will mourn because of Him. Even so, Amen" (Revelation 1:7).

And now we would notice a very striking and unusual type of the resurrection of our Lord,

The Sign of the Prophet Jonah

Certain of the scribes and Pharisees asked a sign from our Lord. They did not ask with any good intention of being persuaded of our Lord's divine commission, but to try to catch Him in His words. Our Lord replied,

> "An evil and adulterous generation seeks after a sign, and no sign will be given to it except the sign of the prophet Jonah. For as Jonah was three days and three nights in the belly of the great fish, so will the Son of Man be three days and three nights in the heart of the earth. The men of Nineveh will rise up in the judgment with this generation and condemn it, because they repented at the preaching of Jonah; and indeed a greater than Jonah is here" (Matthew 12:39-41).

We may well be surprised that Jonah should be chosen by our Lord as a type of Himself. Indeed it would be hard to find two characters so dissimilar as Jonah and our Lord. Jonah was the disobedient prophet, who fled from the presence of the Lord; our Lord was obedient to the will of

God, even to the death of the cross. But our Lord Himself narrowed the sign to one incident in the life of the disobedient prophet, to the time when he was vomited out of the belly of the great fish, and preached to the inhabitants of Nineveh with such remarkable results.

The story is simply told. Nineveh, the capital of Assyria, was the greatest city of the then-known world. To cross it on foot was a three days' journey, so vast was it. We are told it contained over 120,000 souls, who did not know their right hand from their left. But the wickedness of the city was great, and had come up before God. He commanded Jonah, the son of Amittai, to cry against it, and pronounce its doom. Jonah shrank from the task. How could he, an unknown Jew, denounce such a great city? It would be at the peril of his life were he to attempt it. So he rose to flee from the presence of the Lord. Instead of travelling east at the bidding of the Lord, he travelled west in disobedience. He became a passenger in a ship going to Tarshish. Then the Lord caused a mighty tempest to arise, so that the ship was like to be broken. The mariners were afraid, crying every man to his god, and throwing overboard the cargo of the ship to lighten it. Meanwhile Jonah had gone down to the lowest part of the ship, and was fast asleep. Jonah had already told them that he was fleeing from the presence of the Lord. The storm was so threatening that these superstitious mariners cast lots as to why the tempest had arisen, and for whose cause it had come upon them. The lot fell on Jonah.

The sailors then asked Jonah what was to be done. Under enormous pressure, we may be sure, and with a deep sense that God was dealing with him, and that after all there was no chance of escaping from His presence, in utter despair Jonah replied that the one and only remedy was to cast him into the sea, and then it would become calm.

THE SIGN OF THE PROPHET JONAH

The kind-hearted mariners were reluctant to take such a tragic step, and tried their best to bring the ship to land, but without avail.

They were faced with the awful choice of one dying for the many, or the many dying. In either case Jonah would be drowned, they would argue. So the inevitable had to be, and with great reluctance Jonah was flung into the boiling sea, and the sea became calm.

In the east at that time news travelled far and wide in an incredibly short space of time, with unbelievable rapidity. Gossip passed from mouth to mouth, bazaar to bazaar, city to city, country to country. Such a story as this could not fail to excite the liveliest interest. What sort of God was this God of the Hebrews from whom His prophet could not escape, the God who could bring His disobedient servant, as they thought, to such a tragic end? Even the people of Nineveh would surely hear the startling news. When the waters rolled over the head of Jonah, the mariners, and all who afterwards heard the tragic news, would of course come to the conclusion that the prophet was dead, and that this was the last they would hear of him. At the least the news would give the people fresh ideas of the wonderful God of the Hebrews. He would stand out as utterly different from their gods. They would be prepared to pay attention to what message He might send.

Startling as the news was, the like of which had never before been known, in three days' time news of a far more startling and wonderful nature was passed from lip to lip. Jonah was alive and well. Incredible! At first news of this it would be promptly disbelieved as a thing impossible. But there were many witnesses to His being cast into the tempestuous sea. There could be no doubt as to his fate.

Humanly speaking nothing could save him from being drowned. But Jonah was actually alive and well. The God of the Hebrews had ordained a great fish to be at the exact spot when Jonah sank into the water to swallow him, and convey him for three days and nights through the sea, and finally to vomit him alive upon dry land. Here was to them a new and mighty power in the world. It took a lot of believing, but the witnesses to the prophet's supposed death, and the witnesses to the fact that he was alive, and even at that moment carrying out God's commission, and on his way to Nineveh, were so many, that extraordinary as the news was, there was nothing to do but to admit facts.

We know that this story has been the occasion of much derision. Not many years ago, it would have been the occasion of similar scepticism, that people could make a submarine, capable of carrying a crew at the bottom of the sea for a lengthened period of time, and bring them safely to the surface of the sea alive and well. Yet this is a common experience today. And could not God, who created all the fishes by His all-powerful word, create a single fish for the purpose of receiving Jonah as he sank in the waters, and bring him safely to land? Of course He could.

Then the news came that Jonah had actually penetrated into Nineveh a day's journey, uttering fearlessly his message of doom,

> "Yet forty days, and Nineveh shall be overthrown!" (Jonah 3:4).

What did the Ninevites say amongst themselves? They would say surely that if God was so determined to warn them — first by commissioning His servant to deliver the message of doom; second, by sending a mighty tempest to stop His runaway servant; third, by preparing a great fish for his journey under the water; fourth, by directing the fish to vomit Jonah upon dry land; fifth, by giving him courage to proclaim His message in the midst of their great city — surely it was high time that they paid heed to God's warning.

So from the least to the greatest they put on sackcloth and ashes and proclaimed a fast, even the King on his throne divesting himself of his royal robe, clothing himself in sackcloth, and sitting in ashes. God, ever gracious to the repentant, spared the city.

Our Lord drew the contrast between the people of Nineveh repenting at the preaching of Jonah, and the evil and adulterous people who stood before Him, and who were trying to catch Him in His words. He told them plainly that the people of Nineveh would rise in judgment against them, adding

"A greater than Jonah is here."

Our Lord prophesied His own resurrection, that for three days and nights He would be in the heart of the earth, and rise the third day. Was this not far more wonderful than the sudden reappearance of Jonah, believed to be dead, but miraculously preserved in order to give God's message? But our Lord was crucified. He actually died. He was buried. The men who were plotting His death must have known that His resurrection, if it took place, would be the most signal proof by God of His complete satisfaction with all that our Lord died to accomplish. No wonder, when He did die, and the third day of His burial came, the morning of His resurrection, the news of that great event filled the hearts of the scribes and high priests with a terrible fear. If *they* crucified our Lord, and *God* raised Him from the dead, there was a clear and solemn issue between guilty man and a Holy God. The resurrection of our Lord was a visual demonstration that God will judge the living and the dead (Acts 17:31). You and I, whether we like it or not, will have to give account as to how we stand in relation to that resurrection. Thank God, for believers on the Lord Jesus Christ His resurrection is the great proof of their acceptance before God.

Our Lord is risen, alive, living in the power of an endless life, fullest proof indeed of His claims as to His Person, and of the character of His atoning work on the cross. People will do well to pay heed to His message. If the people of Nineveh paid heed to the preaching of Jonah, we can say with a wealth of meaning, of comfort for the believer on the Lord Jesus Christ; but of the strongest, most solemn, warning of coming and eternal judgment to the unbeliever:

"Indeed a greater than Jonah is here."

Were the Four Records of the Resurrection of Christ Inspired?

If the records of the four evangelists were uninspired, we should have found them acting pretty much like present-day newspaper correspondents, trying to emulate each other in the number of details given, and in the recital of strange and startling events. We find a complete absence of any such rivalry in the four Gospels. To compare the four accounts of the events connected with our Lord's resurrection is very interesting. For instance, Matthew does not record the Lord's ascension; Mark gives it in one verse, Luke gives it slightly more fully, adding information as to it in Acts 1:7-11; whilst John does not mention the ascension at all, save that it is implied in the words of our Lord spoken to Peter concerning John,

> "If I will that he remain till I come, what is that to you?" (John 21:23).

Our Lord could not *come* from heaven, unless He had previously *gone* to heaven.

Only Matthew gives us the concocted story of the chief priests that the body of our Lord was stolen by His disciples. Two Gospels give the incident of the two disciples going to Emmaus. Mark refers to it in two verses. Luke gives great detail, running into twenty-three verses. Matthew does not mention our Lord appearing to the eleven disciples, whilst Mark, Luke and John do, this last alone telling of the Lord appearing a *second* time to the eleven, especially mentioning Thomas, surnamed Didymus. Matthew tells us of the eleven disciples meeting the Lord as appointed on a mountain in Galilee. Mark mentions the same appointment, but says nothing of the actual meeting. Luke and John say nothing about it.

John alone gives us the incident of Peter and six other disciples going fishing, and the Lord standing on the shore of the sea of Galilee to receive them with a fire of coals with broiled fish and bread. Mark specially emphasizes the unbelieving attitude of the disciples to the testimony of our Lord's resurrection. See Mark 16:11, 13-14. Of all the evangelists John gives us the fullest account of our Lord's resurrection activities. This is all the more noteworthy seeing the Gospel of John was written more than thirty years after the other Gospels had been in circulation.

We are indebted to the Apostle Paul for further information, not given by the four evangelists. We are told in 1 Corinthians 15 of our Lord's special appearances to the Apostles Peter and James, whilst the former is alluded to in Luke 24:34. He confirms that our Lord saw the eleven disciples twice. It is through Paul alone that we know of the Lord being seen by about five hundred brothers at once.

While two evangelists only give us the account of the virgin birth of our Lord; and two only mention His temptation in the wilderness, and John says not a word about his transfiguration, yet all four evangelists give us in full detail the story of our Lord's sufferings and sacrificial atoning death on the cross of Calvary. This is to be specially noted as of great significance.

One marvels at the restraint put upon the sacred writers by the hand of inspiration. Much, using the phraseology of newspaper correspondents, which would have made "good copy" is not mentioned. For instance the outstanding miracle of the raising to life of Lazarus is only mentioned by John, and is not even alluded to in the synoptic gospels. The accounts given in the four gospels exhibit a realism of unvarnished truth.

THE CONSISTENCY OF TRUTHFULNESS

If a number of people agree to lie and deceive the public, it is very evident that in the nature of things discrepancies and inconsistencies and contradictions would occur in their evidence. It is well-known that in a court of law a clever counsel can extract answers to searching questions, which are fatal to any seeking to cover up the truth.

There is a story told of a little lad being put on oath to give witness in a law case. The opposing counsel contended that he was unreliable as being too young, and probably told by his elders what to say. He then asked the boy, "Did your father tell you what to say?" "Yes, sir," replied the lad. The counsel turned triumphantly to the judge, and said, "You see, my Lord, my contention holds good." "Not quite so fast," replied the judge, and turning to the little lad kindly, he said to him, "Come here, my boy, and tell me what your father told you to say." "Yes, sir," replied the boy, "my father told me to be sure to speak the truth." To the annoyance of the counsel the judge ordered that the evidence of the boy should be taken, which proved to be the obstacle to his winning his case.

THE RESURRECTION OF THE LORD JESUS CHRIST

It has been pointed out that if six witnesses of a fatal accident are called upon to give evidence concerning it, the best proof of their truthfulness would be their *agreeing* on the salient features of the case, but *differing* and even *contradicting* each other, as to details. If they agreed in every detail, it would lead to the suspicion of its being a put-up job, and that the witnesses were instructed to testify in agreement with each other in every little detail.

It is well-known that in witnessing a fatal accident one person sees it a little differently than another. One part of the accident makes a deeper impression than another part. Therefore the absence of uniformity as to details will tend to show, rather than the reverse, the truthfulness of the witnesses.

But in the case of the sacred record regarding the resurrection of our Lord we have two things to point out. First that the four historians, Matthew, Mark, Luke and John, do not furnish us with the same incidents and details as to the resurrection of our Lord, showing, that it is no put-up job; and, second, seeing *the records are inspired*, God-breathed, there are no discrepancies or contradictions.

And so we see the record more or less full in details, one writer mentioning one incident, a second writer, another incident, and yet the accounts fitting perfectly in detail one with the other — no discrepancies, no contradictions. How confirmatory of the truthfulness of the sacred narrative.

The Conversion of the Apostle Paul

We have heard up to now from the witnesses to the resurrection who saw our Lord during the forty days He spent on earth between His resurrection and ascension. Now we bring forward a witness, who, as far as we know, never saw our Lord upon earth; and, if he had, it was as His bitterest enemy, and the persecutor of His people. We refer to the Apostle Paul. In giving a list of those who saw the risen Lord, he finished with himself as a witness, not having seen the Lord when on earth, saying,

> "Then last of all He was seen by me also, as by one born out of due time. For I am the least of the apostles, who am not worthy to be called an apostle, because I persecuted the church of God" (1 Corinthians 15:8-9).

Paul was pressing on his murderous errand to Damascus, armed with authority from the chief priests to drag the Christians to prison, and in some cases to put them to death, when suddenly there shone round his path a light "brighter than the sun". He heard a voice, saying,

"Saul, Saul, why are you persecuting **Me**?" (Acts 9:4).

Up to that moment Paul had sincerely thought that Christ was an impostor, that He was dead and buried, and that he was doing God's service in seeking to stamp Christ's name off the face of the earth. In a moment he recognized that the One who spoke to him from heaven, was none less than the risen glorified Son of God, and that in persecuting the Christians he was in reality persecuting their Lord in glory. Paul saw the Lord, thus qualifying him in one particular to be an apostle, for one mark of an apostle was that he had seen the Lord (Acts 1:21-22). "Out of due time" Paul saw Him as glorified in heaven. His natural sight blinded by the marvellous light brighter than the noonday sun, his dark soul was illuminated with the true knowledge of the Lord. In a moment he was turned from being a bitter persecutor of God's people, poor and afflicted as they were, to being our Lord's most devoted and zealous servant. Note carefully that this all hinged on his discovering the fact of the resurrection of our Lord.

It can safely be affirmed that the conversion of the Apostle Paul was the most remarkable conversion that ever took place in the history of the world. The proof of this statement lies in the following Scripture:

> "This is a faithful saying and worthy of all acceptance, that Christ Jesus came into the world to save sinners, of whom **I am chief**. However, for this reason I obtained mercy, that in me first Jesus Christ might show **all longsuffering**, as a pattern to those who are going to believe on Him for everlasting life" (1 Timothy 1:15-16).

THE CONVERSION OF THE APOSTLE PAUL

Never was there such defiance against Christ displayed as in the case of Paul. He speaks of himself with deep contrition as "a blasphemer, a persecutor, and an insolent man" (1 Timothy 1:13); as "being exceedingly enraged" to the extent of persecuting the Christians "even to foreign cities" (Acts 26:11).

The chief of sinners is in glory. Hallelujah! In him we learn how far God's longsuffering can go. His conversion is a proof to any and every sinner, however degraded or philosophically antagonistic to the Gospel of the grace of God they may be, that the way to life, forgiveness, salvation is open to them. Outside the life of our adorable Lord, which stands infinitely and uniquely beyond every other life, the conversion of the Apostle Paul has made a greater mark on the world through his inspired writings than that of any other man, whether he be eminent in the realm of theology, statesmanship, economics or war.

The Epistle to the Romans written by Paul is a priceless and unique unfolding of the Gospel of the grace of God. His other epistles bring before us assembly truth, and have been the occasion of many gatherings of God's people being formed all over the world from that day to this.

His own activities, till martyrdom ended his faithful service, as narrated in the Acts of the Apostles, show how his own personal efforts were greatly blessed in the spread of the Gospel, and the foundation of Christian fellowship in a wonderful way.

The Testimony of the Epistles to the Resurrection of Christ

We get the resurrection of our Lord detailed in the four gospels. The epistles trace for us the results flowing from the resurrection in the way of doctrines, and their application to Christian living.

To begin with we get the knowledge of salvation linked up very specially with the resurrection of Christ. We read,

> "If you confess with your mouth the Lord Jesus and believe in your heart that *God has raised Him from the dead*, you will be saved" (Romans 10:9).

Again we read,

> "Now it was not written for his [Abraham's] sake alone that it [righteousness] was imputed to him, but also for us. It shall be imputed to us who believe in Him who raised up Jesus our Lord from the dead" (Romans 4:23-24).

Another very striking verse links up the resurrection of our Lord with the raising up of the mortal bodies of the saints, who are alive in the earth at the second coming of

Christ. Ponder over this verse till you grasp its wondrous meaning:

> "If the Spirit of Him who raised Jesus from the dead dwells in you, *He who raised Christ from the dead* will also give life to your mortal bodies through His Spirit who dwells in you" (Romans 8:11).

That is to say, that the Holy Spirit is the power that raised our Lord from the dead: and that same Spirit, indwelling the mortal bodies of the saints, is the pledge that their bodies shall be raised up by the same Power at the coming of the Lord (1 Thessalonians 4:13-18).

Writing to the assembly at Corinth a whole chapter of fifty-eight verses is devoted to an argument proving the value of the resurrection of Christ. We read,

> "If Christ is preached that He has been raised from the dead, how do some among you say that there is no resurrection of the dead? But if there is no resurrection of the dead, then Christ is not risen. And if Christ is not risen, then our preaching is empty and your faith is also empty" (1 Corinthians 15:12-14).

Writing to the assembly at Ephesus we find the same stress put upon the fact of the resurrection of Christ. We read,

> "God, who is rich in mercy, because of His great love with which He loved us, even when we were dead in trespasses, made us alive together with Christ (by grace you have been saved), *and raised us up together*, and made us sit together in the heavenly places in Christ Jesus" (Ephesians 2:4-6).

In this interesting passage we have the *actual* resurrection of our Lord stated, as having a *moral* effect on the believer in so identifying him with the risen Christ, as to put him in spirit on risen ground before God.

Writing to the Philippian assembly we read,

> "And being found in appearance as a man, He humbled Himself and became obedient to the point of death, even the death of the cross. Therefore *God also has highly exalted Him* and given Him the name which is above every name" (Philippians 2:8-9).

Here we have our Lord's resurrection and ascension given as the intimate result of His death on the cross on behalf of sinful people.

Writing to the Thessalonian assembly we read, that they were saved

> "to wait for His Son from heaven, *whom He raised from the dead*, even Jesus who delivers us from the wrath to come" (1 Thessalonians 1:10).

Writing to Timothy, his son in the faith, the Apostle Paul said,

> "Remember that *Jesus Christ, of the seed of David, was raised from the dead* according to my gospel" (2 Timothy 2:8).

The Epistle to the Hebrews ends with a magnificent doxology, in which the resurrection of our Lord is emphasized,

> "Now may the God of peace *who brought up our Lord Jesus from the dead*, that great Shepherd of the sheep, through the blood of the everlasting covenant, make you complete in every good work to do His will, working in you what is well pleasing in His sight, through Jesus Christ, to whom be glory for ever and ever. Amen" (Hebrews 13:20-21).

THE TESTIMONY OF THE EPISTLES TO THE RESURRECTION

The Apostle Peter writes of believers as those,

> "who through Him believe in God, who raised Him [Christ] from the dead and gave Him glory, so that your faith and hope are in God" (1 Peter 1:21).

Besides Scriptures that mention directly the resurrection of our Lord, it is very evident on reading through the epistles of the New Testament that the whole system of Christian teaching is based on the resurrection of our Lord. We give one single example of what we mean,

> "Our citizenship is in heaven, from which we also eagerly wait for the Saviour, the Lord Jesus Christ" (Philippians 3:20).

Though the resurrection is not expressly mentioned in this Scripture, yet it is taken for granted, for if the Saviour is coming from heaven to call His saints into His presence, and He died and was buried, as we know happened to Him, He must have risen from the dead and ascended to glory in order to fulfil this Scripture.

A very good illustration of this is seen in the ocean. When the salt sea recedes from the shore again and again, as tide succeeds tide, salt crystals are formed on the rocks. These are *visible*, yet the salt that forms them, though *invisible* to the naked eye, is in *solution* at all times and in all places of the ocean.

So we have definite proof texts as to the resurrection of Christ blessedly *visible* in the Scriptures, yet the fact of His resurrection is found *in solution*, as it were, throughout the whole of Scripture.

If Scripture had been framed on a lie, this could not have been sustained in perfect consistency throughout the writings of the inspired penmen. Slips, inconsistencies, contradictions would have occurred. Yet not one inconsistency can be discovered, however microscopically the Scriptures are examined. This is most convincing.

Lies and Theories

We shall see how true it is that a lie cannot be consistent when we consider how

THE CHIEF PRIESTS CONCOCTED A LYING TALE

The account that the Roman guard gave of the happenings at the grave was serious hearing indeed. The chief priests were appalled. At all costs the story of the resurrection must be denied. Something must be done, and done quickly to meet the situation. So they concocted a most improbable story. We read,

> "When they [the chief priests] had assembled with the elders and consulted together, they gave a large sum of money to the soldiers, saying, 'Tell them, "His disciples came at night and stole Him away while we slept." And if this comes to the governor's ears, we will appease him and make you secure.' So they took the money and did as they were instructed; and this saying is commonly reported among the Jews until this day" (Matthew 28:12-15).

A true story will hang together, and be capable of being minutely examined. But this tale is far from convincing. If **all** the guard were asleep, how could they know that the disciples had stolen the body? If, further, the body was stolen, how could *sleeping* men know what had become of it? Was **all** the guard likely to be asleep on the morning of the third day when our Lord prophesied He would rise from the dead, especially when they knew that by sleeping at their posts they ran the risk of the death penalty? Of course they could not deny that the stone was rolled away, and the tomb empty. So some story must be told to get out of the difficulty of acknowledging that our Lord had risen from the dead.

Was it likely that the removal of the stone by the disciples, and the carrying away of the body of their Lord, could be carried out so silently and expeditiously that not one of the sleeping guard was awakened? The operation would take considerable time, and be accompanied by noise and force.

And further would "a large sum of money" be given to the guard *to speak the truth*? Did not the largeness of the bribe indicate the extent of the fear that possessed the chief priests, that the truth would eventually come out, and the danger accruing to them in the lies they told be found to be a very real thing?

And if the body had been removed by the disciples, why did the chief priests content themselves with bribing the soldiers to tell a lie, involving them in great risk, and not seek by every possible means to find the body? How convincing it would have been that there was no resurrection of our Lord, if the chief priests could have obtained the body, and publicly exhibited it. That would have settled the matter once and for all. Where was the body? *The body was never produced.* Why? Because there was no dead body, but a living risen Christ.

The story the chief priests concocted would fail to convince any, save those who were willing to be deceived by any improbable tale rather than acknowledge the fact of the resurrection of the One they had crucified with scorn and shame.

THE SWOON THEORY

Another theory of later years has been put forth, that our Lord did not die, but only fainted, that in the quiet and cool of the tomb He had revived, and that what had happened was not the resurrection of a dead Christ, but the resuscitation of a living man.

But this theory will not hold together. There were too many witnesses to His death to render it possible. The centurion, who had charge of the crucifixion; the Roman guard, who carried it out; especially the soldier, who pierced His side; Joseph of Arimathæa and Nicodemus, who brought the body down from the cross, and who would surely have found signs of life, if there had been any — all were witnesses of our Lord's death. There were also the women, who were present at the burial, including those, who loved Him tenderly, and knew Him intimately, among them His own mother according to the flesh.

Moreover, speaking after the manner of a man, was it possible that One, who had gone through the awful experience of crucifixion, and in addition to this had been in the tomb for three days and three nights without food or drink, would be able to release Himself from the linen clothes which tightly bound Him, and then roll back the stone, and disappear in the morning light, in spite of a guard set to watch the tomb? Impossible!

The signs that followed our Lord's death were not consistent with a mere faint. Why should there be a great earthquake; why should the graves in which the bodies of saints lay be opened; why, above all, should the great veil of the Temple be torn in two from the top to the bottom, evidently by the hand of God Himself, if Christ did not die? But all these signs harmonize with the triumph of the Son of God when He rose from the dead, the Victor over sin and death and hell.

THE HALLUCINATION THEORY

Another theory put forth is that, those who professed to see the risen Lord were the subjects of hallucination; that is, they imagined seeing that which did not exist. One can understand it possible for an emotional over-wrought individual, overwhelmed with grief, and in the dim light of the break of day, believing that he or she had seen the Lord, when it was not so. Have we not all imagined trees and shrubs in the dim moonlight taking shape like human beings, when we knew all the time it was only imagination. But our Lord spent no less than forty days on this earth after His resurrection and before His ascension, giving many tangible proofs of the reality of His resurrection.

There were too many witnesses to the fact of the resurrection to make it possible they were all the subjects of hallucination. Our Lord was seen on four occasions by His disciples. They were allowed to see the wounds in His feet and hands and side, even to the length of putting the finger in the prints of the nails. Moreover He ate and drank with them. He walked miles with the two disciples going to Emmaus. He invited His disciples to handle Him, and convince themselves that He was no apparition, that a spirit did not have flesh and bones, as He was seen to have. And even more, the Apostle Paul spoke of five hundred brothers at once seeing Him. Were they all the subjects of hallucination? No, this theory will not stand examination, and can safely be dismissed as another lie of the enemy.

We come now to the consideration of Lord Lyttleton's treatise which we promised to take up in some detail.

Observations on the Conversion and Apostleship of St. Paul

This was the title of a treatise written by Lord Lyttleton to which we have previously referred. We will now bring forward some of his arguments, the answer to which convinced himself against his disbelief that the conversion of the Apostle Paul was real.

We will take the key points of his arguments, putting them in our own words. We may mention that the treatises written by Lord Lyttleton and his friend, Gilbert West, can be seen today in the Bodleian Library, Oxford and are widely available on the internet.

The actual conversion of the Apostle Paul is described in Acts 9, and further the Apostle himself twice narrated it, first when he addressed the fanatical crowd from the castle stairs at Jerusalem, and again when he stood before King Agrippa to answer for himself.

Lord Lyttleton took up four points of view for examination:

(1) *Either Paul was an impostor, who said what he knew to be false, with intent to deceive;* or
(2) *He was an enthusiast, who misled himself by the force of an over-heated imagination;* or
(3) *He was deceived by the fraud of others;* or finally
(4) *What he declared to be the occasion of his conversion did really happen, and therefore the Christian religion is a divine revelation.*

In the consideration of these points of view, we begin by asking,

(1) Was Paul an Imposter?

Every reader of this pamphlet must have had some experience of impostors at some time or other. There comes along the sneaking, ingratiating person, a plausible teller of lies, seeking to gain some sordid advantage, which may be of money or position or power. Let us see what advantage Paul could hope to gain by imposture.

(A) Was it wealth that Paul sought?

We all know that some upstarts get great wealth by their propaganda; for instance, Mrs. Eddy of Christian Science fame, whose royalties on her books made her a millionaire. It was far otherwise with the Apostle Paul. If he had remained religiously a Jew, he was on the high road to a place of great distinction among his nation. With such a position there would have come great ease of circumstances. But once converted to the Christian faith, he turned his back upon these tempting prospects, and took up the cause of the humble Christians, poor and persecuted as they were.

He sometimes worked with his own hands night and day at tent-making to provide bare necessities for himself and co-workers in the Gospel field. The whole record of his life, as given in the Acts of the Apostles, supports the claim he made to the Ephesian elders:

> "I have coveted no one's silver or gold or apparel. Yes, you yourselves know that these hands have provided for my necessities, and for those who were with me. I have shown you in every way, by labouring like this, that you must support the weak. And remember the words of the Lord Jesus, that He said, 'It is more blessed to give than to receive'" (Acts 20: 33-35).

At the end of his life see him a prisoner for the Gospel's sake at Rome, chained to a soldier, awaiting martyrdom at the hands of Nero, the cruellest of the Roman Emperors, begging Timothy to bring him a cloak, for he was shivering in the severity of an Italian winter. Is this the life, are these the actions, of an impostor? Throughout the whole of Paul's record there shines a truthfulness, a sincerity, a transparency, that is quite inconsistent with the idea of imposture.

(B) WAS IT A GREAT REPUTATION THAT PAUL WAS SEEKING?

What reputation could Paul expect from a nation that had, with fanatical hatred, rejected and crucified the Son of God, whom, after conversion, he straightway proclaimed as such in the very stronghold of the Jewish religion? Nor would he fare any better with the Gentiles, the pagans, who worshipped idols, as witness the uproar in which he was embroiled when the silversmith of Ephesus, who made silver shrines for the goddess Diana, declared that their craft was in danger if the Christian religion was allowed to take root. To "preach Christ crucified" was "to the Jews a stumbling block and to the Greeks foolishness" (1 Corinthians 1:23). Would such preaching bring him reputation?

He tells us himself that God has chosen the foolish things of the world to put to shame the wise, the weak things to put to shame the mighty, the base things, the things which are despised, and the things that are not, to bring to nothing the things that are (1 Corinthians 1:27-28). This was the circle in which Paul chose to move. He certainly did not seek a place in a world which had crucified His Lord.

(C) WAS IT POWER PAUL WAS SEEKING?

This has often been the urge with many, who have put forth religious claims, and along with them sought worldly power and influence. Take the case of the popes of Rome during the middle ages. They were marked by political ambition, straining every nerve for secular power, aiming to be in a position to dictate to the proudest rulers of the day. Is this not alas! largely true at this present time? How vastly different was the conduct of the Apostle Paul. You never find him striving to be the head of a party, or interfering with politics, or inciting people to rebellion, hoping thereby to obtain for himself reputation and power.

His attitude to the world is clearly defined:

> "Let every soul be subject to the governing authorities. For there is no authority except from God, and the authorities that exist are appointed by God. Therefore whoever resists the authority resists the ordinance of God, and those who resist will bring judgment on themselves" (Romans 13:1-2).

When it was the case of his religious association, where he might have sought to gain great pre-eminence and power as a religious leader, we see clearly that this was not so, as witness his conduct when he rebuked division making in the assembly at Corinth. Suppressing the names of the actual division makers, and introducing the names of Peter and Apollos and his own, in their persons he rebuked the emerging heresies (1 Corinthians 4:6). We read:

> "Now I say this, that each of you says, 'I am of Paul,' or 'I am of Apollos,' or 'I am of Cephas,' or 'I am of Christ.' Is Christ divided? Was Paul crucified for you? Or were you baptized in the name of Paul?" (1 Corinthians 1:12-13).

If it had been power that Paul was seeking, he could not have rebuked these Corinthian leaders, who were seeking it, by rebuking it in his own person. Read the record of his life as seen in the Acts of the Apostles, and as witnessed by his epistles, and you will find no trace of seeking after power.

(D) WAS PAUL'S MOTIVE THE GRATIFICATION OF SOME OTHER PASSION?

It is well-known that religious fanatics, who arise periodically only to disappear in public disgrace, sometimes pretend to a divine revelation as a means of indulging in the gratification of their desires for luxurious living, and often for that of immoral conduct. In England, in the late nineteenth century, the Anglican founders of Agapemone (Greek, *love abode*) were a set of religious visionaries with unedifying ideas about sexual relations, and who were denounced by all decent people. And yet this was under the shadow of religion. In the latter part of the twentieth century, in the USA, cults led by Jim Jones and David Koresh followed a similar, though more violent, pattern.

Read the writings of the Apostle Paul, and you will not find a trace of this. No scandal was ever recorded in connection with his name. Hear his strong warning on the subject, needed today more than ever:

> "Therefore be imitators of God as dear children. ... But fornication and all uncleanness or covetousness, let it not even be named among you, as is fitting for saints; neither filthiness, nor foolish talking, nor coarse jesting, which are not fitting, but rather giving of thanks. For this you know, that no fornicator, unclean person, nor covetous man, who is an idolater, has any inheritance in the kingdom of Christ and God" (Ephesians 5:1-5).

These were his sentiments. You cannot accuse Paul of seeking to find in his conversion the means for the gratification of the sins of the flesh.

(E) WAS THE ACCOUNT OF PAUL'S CONVERSION A PIOUS FRAUD ON HIS PART?

If his conversion had been a fraud, we might have imagined that he would have located the occurrence in some remote inaccessible spot, where there could be no witnesses to refute his statements. Instead of this he tells us more than once that his conversion occurred quite close to the famous city of Damascus, in the full glare of the mid-day sun, in the presence of a retinue, which must have consisted of a considerable number of persons. They saw the blinding light, above that of the mid-day sun, they heard the voice, not understanding the words. They could have contradicted Paul's story, if it had been untrue.

Nor could he have fabricated the story in collaboration with the Christians, when he was their bitterest enemy, and occupied at the time of his conversion in searching for them to bring them to prison and sometimes to death. Instead of collaborating they kept out of his way in mortal fear.

Then further, how could it be accounted for that a man, approaching Damascus as a bitter opponent of the Christians, entered it to become a most devoted servant of the Lord. Never was a conversion more outstanding. His position of being empowered by authority of the chief priests was known to the whole nation, and his sudden conversion, and complete reversal of his sympathies and actions, must have made a great impression upon the whole nation, so much so that he could say, when he stood before King Agrippa,

> "The king, before whom I also speak freely, knows these things; for I am convinced that none of these things escapes his attention, since this thing was not done in a corner" (Acts 26:26).

Could Paul have so addressed the king, if his conversion was not well-known to him, before whom he stood as a prisoner?

If the assertion of his conversion had been fraudulent, then was the occasion for King Agrippa to have said so. On the contrary he exclaimed,

> "You almost persuade me to become a Christian" (Acts 26:28).

Never did the great Apostle of the Gentiles appear to greater advantage than when he replied to the king with power and earnestness:

> "I would to God that not only you, but also all who hear me today, might become both *almost* and **altogether** such as I am, except for these chains" (Acts 26:29).

Did this look like a pious fraud on his part? Does it not ring grandly true? Only wilfully blind persons could think otherwise.

And perhaps the strongest answer to our question is found in Paul's subsequent career after his conversion. Would a man give himself to a life of austerity and privation and danger for the propagation of a lie? Look at the persecutions he endured — the scourgings, imprisonments, ending in martyrdom. Look at the work he did: the converts he made: the assemblies he formed. Hear his own words forced out of him in self-defence, wrung from him unwillingly, for speaking of himself was most distasteful to him. He wrote:

> "Are they ministers of Christ? — I speak as a fool — I am more: in labours more abundant, in stripes above measure, in prisons more frequently, in deaths often. From the Jews five times I received forty stripes minus one. Three times I was beaten with rods; once I was stoned; three times I was shipwrecked; a night and a day I have been in the deep; in journeys often, in perils of waters, in perils of robbers, in perils of my own countrymen, in perils of the Gentiles, in perils in the city, in perils in the wilderness, in perils in the sea, in perils among false brethren; in weariness and toil, in sleeplessness often, in hunger and thirst, in fastings often, in cold and nakedness — besides the other things, what comes upon me daily: my deep concern for all the churches" (2 Corinthians 11:23-28).

Think well over this amazing list. How would you like to be stripped to the waist, and feel the dull thud of the whip cutting into your flesh again and again, whilst the blood flowed freely from a dozen gaping wounds. And this is what this refined scholarly servant of Christ had to endure again and again. Was this all done for the propagation of a lie? Was his teaching, emphasizing truthfulness, cleanness of life, self-denial, merely a cover for depths of corruption and deception? Can it be? With one voice we affirm that such a life does not cover a lie, but was a proof of the reality of the uplift and power of Christianity.

(2) Was Paul an enthusiast, who was led to believe sincerely what was false through an over-heated imagination?

The more we enquire into Paul's conduct and teaching, the more will we be guided to a right conclusion in this matter. Let us begin by asking

(a) Was Paul marked by great heat of temper?

If he were, it might lead to an overheated imagination. The answer to our question is found in the fact that in the record of Paul's life as given in the Acts of the Apostles, you will find nothing but sanity marking the apostle; no sudden emotional outbursts, no wild exhibitions of temper are in evidence, and he had plenty to try his patience.

It is true that he could be vehement when the occasion called for it, for instance when he denounced in no unmeasured terms the Judaising work of men, who sought to corrupt the pure Gospel of the grace of God, but there was no unbalanced heat of temper exhibited, but solemn denunciation in the severest terms, which the occasion demanded.

(b) Was it melancholy that marked Paul, which might have led to self-deception?

Melancholia is described as a form of insanity, producing great depression of mind. How often has the writer met such cases, men and women, who imagined all kinds of depressing things that never happened, but were the fruits of a morbid imagination. But there is no trace of this in Paul's career, no trace of it in his numerous writings.

When cast unjustly into the inner prison at Philippi, with his feet fast in the stocks, his back sore and bleeding with the cruel beating he had received at the hands of the brutal jailor, what was he doing at the midnight hour? Was he wringing his hands, bemoaning his sad fate, imagining all sorts of things? No, he and his companion were occupied in praying to God, and singing His praises, the prisoners hearing them. No signs of melancholia there!

At the end of his career, when he would, if ever, have been disillusioned, how do we find him? As a prisoner at Rome, chained to a soldier, with the prospect of martyrdom just ahead, in what strain did he write to the church at Philippi? Was there any mark of melancholia observable? No, he wrote,

> "Finally, my brethren, rejoice in the Lord" (Philippians 3:1).

* * * * *

> "Rejoice in the Lord always. Again I will say, rejoice!" (Philippians 4:4).

And between these two points in his career we find no trace of melancholia marking him, but rather the characteristics of a sane sober man, gladly yielding all that he had, even to life itself, for the glory of God and the advancement of His kingdom.

The prospect of death left him unmoved and serene, even rejoicing. He wrote,

> "My earnest expectation and hope [is] that in nothing I shall be ashamed, but with all boldness, as

always, so now also Christ will be magnified in my body, whether by life or by death. For to me, to live is Christ, and to die is gain" (Philippians 1:20-21).

Does this sound like melancholy? Are these words those of an impostor, or of the victim of self-deception?

(C) WAS IT IGNORANCE THAT LED PAUL TO DECEPTION?

Ignorance could not have been successfully charged against Paul. He was brought up in Tarsus, Cilicia, in good circumstances apparently, for his father being a Roman citizen was able to pass on this distinction to his son. When the chief captain, mentioned in Acts 22:28, exclaimed that with a great price he had bought this honour, Paul replied that he was free born.

As he grew up to manhood, for the purpose of his rabbinical training he was sent to Jerusalem to be educated under the teaching of the celebrated Gamaliel. There is a saying in the Jewish Talmud, "Since Rabbin Gamaliel has died, the glory of the law has ceased." That Paul was thus educated, strengthens the belief that his father was a man of some affluence.

Paul's education stands in great contrast to that of the Jewish apostles, who were described as "uneducated and untrained men" (Acts 4:13). He was the complete master of two languages, and had received the best education the Jewish nation could furnish. His writings in their clearness and reasoning powers are sufficient to prove that it was not ignorance that led Paul to deception.

(D) WAS IT CREDULITY THAT LED PAUL INTO BELIEVING WHAT WAS NOT TRUE?

Credulity is described as a readiness to believe on improbable grounds. This is ever a mark of opponents to the Bible that they are ready to believe anything that can set aside the Scriptures, such as the "swoon theory", or the "hallucination theory". It has been put forward that Paul's conversion was due to an epileptic fit, as if any person so affected would profess to have seen what Paul saw. It has been said that if Paul's conversion was due to an epileptic fit, it is a great pity that tens of thousands more were not subject to fits of that kind.

What was Paul's condition before conversion? He must have been well aware of our Lord's claims to Deity, His entrance to Manhood's estate. He must have been familiar with stories of the miraculous healings that followed our Lord wherever He went. He must have heard something of His teaching. He knew about the crucifixion. But he was incredulous as to all these things. He believed Christ to be an impostor. He thought that he was actually doing God's service in persecuting with ardour the saints of God. This was his condition of mind when he set forth that morning on his journey of persecuting zeal to Damascus.

When his conversion took place he had no opportunity of speaking to Christians, nor would they have spoken to him, even if he had wished them to do so, for they were extremely afraid of his persecuting rage. It was the amazing discovery, that the One he saw, and who spoke to him from heaven, was Jesus, the Son of God. In a moment of time the great change took place, and his faith did not rest on credulity, but on indisputable grounds. Credulity could not be laid to his charge.

(E) WAS PRIDE OR SELF-SATISFACTION THE CAUSE OF PAUL'S SUDDEN CHANGE OVER?

There have been many instances where excessive pride and self-satisfaction have marked religious leaders, but they have always been to their undoing. Instead of looking at things in due proportion, inordinate ideas of themselves throw everything out of right perspective. There is no trace of this in the Apostle Paul. When the church at Corinth was questioning his authority as Apostle of the Gentiles, he was forced to speak of himself in self-defence. Was it like vanity or self-conceit when he wrote to the church at Corinth,

> "*I have become a fool in boasting; you have compelled me.* For I ought to have been commended by you; for in nothing was I behind the most eminent apostles, *though I am nothing*" (2 Corinthians 12:11).

You can discern in these words what pain it gave the Apostle to have to speak thus of himself. In another place he said he was "less than the least of all the saints" (Ephesians 3:8), as he thought of the days of his persecuting frenzy.

AN UNFORGETTABLE EXPERIENCE

And, what is still more remarkable, he tells us of an experience, the like of which was never known before nor since. In 2 Corinthians 12:1-5 he tells how he was caught up to the third heaven, not knowing, so intense was the bliss of his experience, whether he was in the body or not; and that he heard unspeakable words, not lawful to utter on earth. Of this wonderful experience he wrote,

> "And lest I should be exalted above measure by the abundance of the revelations, a thorn in the flesh was given to me, a messenger of Satan to buffet me, lest I be exalted above measure. Concerning this thing I pleaded with the Lord three times that it might depart from me. And He said to me, 'My grace is sufficient for you, for My strength is made perfect in weakness.' Therefore most gladly I will

rather boast in my infirmities, that the power of Christ may rest upon me" (2 Corinthians 12:7-9).

And what was still more remarkable, he had kept this surpassingly wonderful experience secret for fourteen years, and only mentioned it when driven to do so in rebutting the attack on his God-given apostleship. Was this like pride or self-satisfaction? Far be the thought!

(3) WAS PAUL DECEIVED BY OTHERS?

The answer to this can be put into very few words.

(A) IT WAS **MORALLY** IMPOSSIBLE FOR PAUL TO BE DECEIVED BY OTHERS.

Two conditions in the circumstances attending Paul's conversion show the impossibility of his being deceived by others. First of all, those who accompanied him on the journey to Damascus were of his retinue, and of his own way of thinking, that is in full sympathy with the task of persecuting the Christians, and seeking to stamp the name of Christ from off the face of the earth. Therefore they would be the last persons in the world to suggest the sudden change conversion involved. The second consideration is that the conversion was so perfectly unexpected and sudden, that the change, from being a bitter hater of Christ, to becoming His devoted servant, could not possibly be brought about by the deceitful influence of others.

(B) IT WAS **PHYSICALLY** IMPOSSIBLE FOR PAUL TO BE DECEIVED BY OTHERS.

We have already replied to this when we pointed out that the persons with him would be the last persons in the world to turn him aside from his murderous errand to Damascus. Nor could the Christians have persuaded him, for they were not on the spot, but would have hidden themselves in terror from his persecuting zeal.

(4) Paul's after-life proved the reality of his conversion.

The record of his activities, as seen in the Acts of the Apostles and by the perusal of his remarkable epistles, exhibit a devotion to Christ that shines resplendently; a courage that braved dangers to life and limb continually; an endurance that stood the strain of constant travel in days when travel was arduous and attended with dangers by land and sea. There surely never was a life more devoted to our Lord than his. In this way his conversion and after-life were all of a piece. Such a presentation of Christ in glory as he beheld would make a deep and abiding effect on Paul's waking and sleeping all through the years of his arduous life of labour for the Lord.

If his alleged conversion had never taken place, and he knew it had not, is it conceivable there should flow from the pen of an utterly dishonest man, a stream of ministry upholding righteousness, holiness and truth, presenting the knowledge of God and of Christ, condemning in no measured terms untruthfulness, covetousness, immorality, not only in outward deed but in inward thought? Surely such a thought must be dismissed at once as so utterly incongruous as to be most patently untrue.

One realizes as never before the wisdom of Lord Lyttleton's choice of subject, we believe unwittingly on his part, but surely the overruling hand of God, that in the conversion of Paul we have the last and most powerful witness to the resurrection of Christ, and in his after-life the evidence of how this great truth gripped this truly great man, revolutionizing his life, and affording us a picture of what God can do with a life wholly devoted to Him.

We rise from our study, fully sharing Lord Lyttleton's conclusions, that Paul's conversion was just as the Scripture narrative presents it, and that his conversion and after-life were the greatest events that ever happened in this world, outside the incomparably blessed life and atoning death of our Lord. No events, outside of our Lord's life, have made a greater mark on this world, and even then the life of the Apostle Paul was in reality the life of Christ in measure through a human vessel. The Apostle Paul today under God is shaping the thoughts and lives of millions of the human race, putting into the shade every other influence affecting man's destinies. Christianity is the one and only truly purifying agency in the world today. Let people give up their belief in the Bible, and you find evil rampant, sin unabashed, and the descent of mankind to the level of the beast, and even worse, more evident.

The Bible is putting its mark upon millions of the human race, and indirectly has affected society generally with some sense of decent living. Out of twenty-one inspired epistles we have in the New Testament no less than fourteen come from the pen of the Apostle Paul. To put it another way, out of 3,601 verses no less than 2,767 of them come from his pen, whilst only 834 verses come from the pens of the remaining writers of inspired epistles.

The truth that Paul covered in his written ministry is very impressive — the truth of the Gospel of the grace of God in all its fullness; the unfolding of the truth of the church of God as the mystical body of Christ, of which He is the glorious Head in heaven; Christians being indwelt by the Holy Spirit of God; the truth as to the Lord's second coming, and His appearing to set up His kingdom on earth, with which for the Christian is connected the teaching as to the judgment seat of Christ. All this and more covers ground beyond what the other epistles set forth. Paul was the Apostle to the Gentiles to whom was communicated the double ministry of the Gospel and of the church.

Is this the record of a deceiver, or a man capable of being deceived by others? Far be the thought!

The Best Authenticated Fact in All History

If the writer had any doubts concerning the fact of the resurrection of our Lord Jesus Christ from the dead, the examination of Scripture on this subject, necessary for the writing of this pamphlet, would have dispelled them all. Not that he had previously any doubt whatever, but the survey of Scripture is so convincing that it left him wondering how a fact so fully proved by competent witnesses, and especially having been prophesied long centuries before the event took place, could ever have been doubted. It has demonstrated to him more than ever the unique character of the resurrection of our Lord, and that the whole scheme of Christianity hinges upon it.

And further, the impact that Christianity has made upon the world, the beauty of individual Christian lives, the power that resides in the Word of God as living and powerful, the fact that it has been translated in whole or in part into over two thousand languages, and is the world's best seller today, all tell us that the fountain, from which for centuries such a stream of blessing has been and is still flowing, must be a pure fountain, truthful and holy and divine.

We can now see still more clearly how everything hinges on the resurrection of Christ. If His assertion that He was the eternal Son of God, the eternal Word, was not true, God would not have raised Him from the dead. If it was not true that He was the eternal Son of God, then the claim to this would have been blasphemy of the very worst kind. Would God have raised a blasphemer? Surely not. Yet He raised Christ from the dead, proving that His claim to be the Son of God was true. If His claim to be the sent One of the Father, to be "the Word become flesh" (John 1:14) was not true, God would not have raised Him from the dead. Would God have raised a blasphemer? Surely not. Yet He raised Christ from the dead, proving that His claim to be "the Word become flesh" was true in the sight of heaven. If our Lord's life had been marred by one sinful thought, word, or deed, God could not have raised Him from the dead, for Christ would then have been a sinner needing a Saviour. But God raised Him from the dead, proving the sinlessness of His earthly life. When our Lord died on the cross He claimed His death to be the fulfilment of the Father's will, an atoning, sacrificial, vicarious death, necessary for the vindication of God's glory, and the salvation of sinful man. With His latest breath our Lord cried with a loud voice,

"It is finished!"

If this had not been blessedly true, God could not have raised Him from the dead. But He was raised by the glory of the Father, showing that heaven fully recognized the character of our Lord's death on the cross, the pledge of salvation to the believing sinner, so we read:

> "He was delivered for our offences, *and was raised again for our justification*" (Romans 4:25, KJV).

It will be thus seen that the Godhead glory of our Lord, His spotless humanity, His atoning death on the cross, and His resurrection, this last being the fullest acknowledgment of heaven of every claim that our Lord made concerning Himself when here on earth, form one indissoluble whole. Everything about our Lord stands or falls together.

We cannot do better in closing what we have to say on this vital matter than repeat the truly magnificent words of Holy Scripture (Romans 6:4):

> **"Christ was raised from the dead
> by** *the glory of the Father.*"

These words stand in all their magnificence and depth of meaning.

THE RESURRECTION OF THE LORD JESUS CHRIST

Other Books from Scripture Truth Publications

Understanding Christianity series:

"Comforted of God" by A J Pollock (editor)
ISBN 978-0-901860-63-7 *(paperback)*
110 pages; April 2010

Understanding the Old Testament Series:

The Tabernacle's Typical Teaching by A J Pollock
ISBN 978-0-901860-65-1 *(paperback)*
236 pages; July 2009

www.ingramcontent.com/pod-product-compliance
Lightning Source LLC
Chambersburg PA
CBHW061339040426
42444CB00011B/2995